Astrology Explained

The Ultimate Astrology Guide for Beginners

Astrology Overview, Basics of Astrology, Zodiac Signs, History, Elements, Proficiency, How to Apply During Reading, and More!

By Riley Star

Foreword

Astrology is a disciplined study that has been present for millions and millions of years which not only intrigued men and women of history but continues to fascinate men and women of today living in the present. This is a subject that deals with the stars, planets and their celestial dance of movements which co-relates to events on the earth and on affairs specific to individual humans.

The study of astrology reaches in further. It is a study on how the position of the planets and stars at the time and date of one's birth, along with the sun and the moon, and how these relate to an individual's life. It is not a magic mirror wherein you can look into and predict where someone or something is. Unfortunately many have come to see astrology to be comical as such because of the many charlatans who set out to make money off the despair of some. Discover the foundational principles of astrology and understand why so many people living today's world are still enthralled by this study despite of many skeptics over the years.

Table of Contents

Introduction

Mankind, for as long as we had become conscious of our own presence on this planet, has been fascinated by the heavens and has been compelled to look up when in search for meaning. Man has historically looked to the skies and the stars, the planets, the moon and the sun for answers. As the most intelligent form of life on this blue dot in the universe, early humans who observed the heavens came to understand that the celestial bodies and objects suspended in the heavens had a correlation with life here on Earth. We learnt the art of learning so that we could find answers and become solution providers. Astrology has taught us that by looking for consistencies in the heavens, we could, to a certain measure, allow man to foretell things. It opened up so many sorts of questions by thinkers, philosophers, intellectuals. These are just some of the undermined aspects of why the invention and investigations of astronomy is important.

Looking up, early man came to understand revelations that knowing the map of the stars in the sky would not only take her home it could help bring her to a place strange and new. That they held positions in the sky which if you recognized would tell you where you are and if you followed, could guide you to where you intend to be. With the bountiful beauty of the heavens it is difficult not to be enthralled and drawn to it. The secrets and magnificence it reveals and hides, all at once permits it the mystery that it is whilst allowing us to skim over an expanse of knowledge that we have yet to discover.

However, early astrologers are to be given credit for looking up longer and harder because they observed the heavens with thoughtful care, and soon after started recording these celestial shifts and movements; the dance of the planets and the stars in the heavens which allowed man to get imaginative, creative but more so, stir the desire for knowledge. Early astrologers are to be credited for allowing mankind to learn about measuring time, gauging the seasons of a year, and other things which shall be revealed to you as you read further.

Bygone kingdom's, courts of yore and governments of late and recent times have, in one way or another, consulted the heavens, often times by means of astrologers, for advice and guidance. Those who had a deeper sense of comprehension of the alignment and/or separation of these celestial objects were sought after for consultation. Astrology was regarded as a science at some point in far history but lost its bearings along the way. And we think that is why you are here; to know the truth about astrology, what it is about and how it relates to us as our daily lives unfold.

You are here to discover what it is and how you can find the accuracy in what has been referred to as a pseudo-science. Do allow us then to take you to the skies as we give you more insight into the deeper and inner studies of astrology and how it ties to us, as individuals, as pairs, events in our lives. Let's look at how the stars and planets and how they relate to the events on this plane as we delve into the mystical and fascinating study of astrology.

Chapter One: Understanding Astrology

The discipline of astrology has been widely misunderstood for so long by so many that the mounting years of misguided information have confused a great multitude of people. So much so that it's real essence has lost the spark in some people's hearts and minds. We hope to re-enlighten you of the realities and truths of these fascinating studies of the celestial alignments relating to their explanation about you and individuals around you, because that is what astrology is. It's focuses more about the explanation of yourself in relation to the positions of Sun and Moon as well as the planetary and star clusters which affect your tides.

My Take on Astrology

Astrology is a subject which requires time and intensive study of the stars and the planets in correlation to the events specific to individual lives and times. It is a skill which requires discipline and structure which may just take a few years to study but requires years to master and continued practice to get better from level to next higher level. Should anyone profess to be a true astrologist and give you step by step directions on what to do about a problem is not at all what any self-respecting astrologer would do. Astrology is not a tool or method to make predictions about the future. Nor is it a portal to look at a person's past. Instead what astrology does is reveal the placements of all these celestial bodies at any certain point and time in a person's life

A real astrologer would make no claims of being able to give you the answer for the next winning numbers of the lottery or who's cheating with whom. Any decent astrologer would not make claims on the absolute accuracy of their "answers". Astrology is not one person's intuition seemingly better than yours, therefore is given the ability to see a vivid picture of the future. No self-respecting astrologer can make claims of being able to foretell anything in detailed accuracy.

Existence in these days of technologically-advanced, science-driven, quick-facts world we live wherein astrology is often written off as a mockery to conclusive facts, we aim to help you find out what the ancients found fascinating about this study. Wet your appetite a tad more than your usual dose of your daily horoscope from the page across the funnies and delve a little deeper into a subject that has captured the mind and curiosity of mankind whether they be believers of the discipline or otherwise.

What is Astrology?

Astrology is a mathematical study of the placement and alignment of the planets, and how the pull of the Sun and the Moon on the Earth along with its pull of the stars and planets affects and affects one's birth date and time. It is a discipline and one that requires technical solving skills as well as rapt attention to detail. It is a methodology that had not only been present in the recent past, it is not an outdated fad, nor is it just a passing fancy. Astrology is a disciplined study that has been present for millions and millions of years which not only intrigued men and women of history but continues to fascinate men and women of today living in the present. This is a subject that deals with the stars, planets and their celestial dance of movements which co-relates to events on the earth and on affairs specific to individual humans.

We owe it to astrology that calendars were invented allowing us to mark and remember milestones, events, what had happened and what to look forward to. Time was given human measure allowing us to go about and organize our days no matter how trivially unimportant a task may have seemed. Aside from that people of the distant past were given clues to understand the changes of the season empowering us (early humans) to establish the best times to sow and reap vital food crops. All these are important revelations, which paved the way for human progress, became established when man started studying the heavens and began mapping out the minor and major shifts of the celestial objects in the sky

Sadly, one trend is apparent; astrology has been watered down to horoscope readings that randomly pop up on your computer screens. The horoscope you read is basically your Sun sign and not much more. These are the generalizations that astrology is about, but it is much deeper and more complex than the generalization of your generated daily horoscope. And because it has been trivialized as such, astrology has become a largely misunderstood topic that has been called many things from hogwash to ridiculous.

On the other hand, reading your daily horoscope is hopefully a good springboard from which you become more curious about the truth about astrology, because it is much more than wasted space on your computer screen or your favorite daily spreadsheet. A horoscope reading should be treated more like a enlightening if not cautionary phrase of wisdom to guide a person. That is how one should treat their horoscope.

The study of astrology reaches in further. It is a study on how the position of the planets and stars at the time and date of one's birth, along with the sun and the moon, and how these relate to an individual's life. It is the alignment, or contrary, of the stars and the planets to the sun, the moon and the earth. When accurately done, a thought out chart gives one insight and empowers you to explain your place in the bigger scheme of things given the set of guidelines which position these celestial parameters, at any given time.

The planets are basically indicators of where we are in the bigger picture. It does not attempt to be a forbearer of future events, nor is it a crystal ball which "shows" what is hidden and you want revealed. It is not a one-size-fits-all, unless generalizations like "it was a good time to be born" is the answer. What astrology does is it narrows down and relates to each individual even more when consideration is taken upon the 12 signs of the zodiac, each with their own combination of the 4 Element qualities unique to a sign.

Astrology is quite like a mathematical philosophy of that aids in explaining life as we know it. It is not a predictive method or talent that gives you or me the ability to foretell the future. And so there is another red flag for you to spot a person with fraudulent credentials posing as an astrologer. No self-respecting astrologer will profess to be able to tell you what lies ahead.

It is not a magic mirror wherein you can look into and predict where someone or something is, nor should it be regarded as a Magic 8 Ball. Unfortunately many have come to see astrology to be comical as such because of the many charlatans who set out to make money off the despair of some. How do you find a real, honest to goodness astrologer? Where do you begin looking? How to tell if you have found the right one? Those are questions we aim to answer with the next segment.

Chapter Two: The Foundation of Astrology

Astrology was once heralded as a science is now relegated to pop culture and regarded as historically erroneous ideas. But its lasting power of lure through thousands of millennia has proven that it has been in the heart and soul of humans to search the sky for answers. Predating all formal disciplinary academics, astrology had given birth to many other disciplines, theories, philosophy and ideas which are in wide practice today. Discover the foundational principles of astrology and understand why despite skeptics of the study so many people living today's world are still enthralled by it.

A Brief History of Astrology

We wouldn't have the disciplines and principles of physics, or astronomy if not for the discovery and observant recordings of early heaven gazing astrologers. Those who first looked up to the skies have essentially inspired these branches of science hence the continued reference to the discipline was heard of throughout time until today. Some of the greatest minds, innovators, scientists, alchemists, theorists, politicians, generals, rulers and commoners alike have had their eyes drawn up to the heavens figuring there must be something out there that makes us make sense.

Lauded to be a scholarly discipline, astrology was once widely accepted as a science alongside astronomy. Astrology was an often used tool to predict weather patterns and seasonal changes. It allowed people to predict weather changes according to the cycles of the year, it also allowed for early farmers to gain better harvest. In effect looking up at the sky and figuring out the

It was the Babylonians who had come up and introduced the discipline of astrology which was later, in 4 BC, picked up by the Greeks. The principles of astrology were then soon inducted into the lives of Romans and it was them who came up with the 12 signs which are used to this day in horoscopes.

Egypt later came up with the zodiac signs and taken up by the Babylonians. The Egyptians recognized the relationship of the 12 constellations to changes in the seasons of each year.

The 12 signs are subdivided into 4 groups which are earth, fire, water and air. Libra, Gemini and Aquarius fall under the sign of Air; Leo, Sagittarius, Aries fall under the Fire sign; Pisces, Cancer, Scorpio fall under the Water sign and Virgo, Taurus, Capricorn make up the Earth sign. We will get into the individual character traits a more as we go along.

Each of these quadrants is housed around a circle. The separation of the 12 houses is founded on Earth's daily motion. All these come into play on circumstances like travel, partnerships, money, relationships etc. While the division of the 12 signs of the zodiac, on the other hand, is founded on the earth's annual rotation around the Sun.

How to Tell Frauds from Real Astrologers

When people are anxious, when they are in trouble, when they feel lost and need immediate answers, and especially out of desperation, people mistakenly turn to natal astrology chart readings to find out if they can get quick results and fast answers to their woes. These are some reasons why so many hack jobs and fraudsters have been able, and continue, to trick people out of their hopes and money. Because con artists have honed their crafty ways, many have fallen victim to and have been turned off from the study altogether, detected by the thought of it being an elaborately orchestrated, hocus pocus scheme.

Astrology is not a quick boost of instant information where answers can be immediately obtained. Nor is it a mere piece of paper inside of a fortune cookie with usually vague ill-translated messages. It is an art, a discipline, if you must, that takes many years to learn and even many years more to master. An astrologist, true to the discipline's principles and foundation has a strong desire for the betterment enlightenment and to further the good reputation of the study. A skilled and thoughtful astrologer is aimed at presenting the truth according to the subject precepts behind what, to the novice, looks to be inconclusive, vague and inaccurate.

A true-blue astrologer would have gone to school to learn the intricacies of the discipline as well as the principal methodologies. It would have taken them a few years of getting educated on the mathematical science of the study and even a longer and on-going period of constant practice. Those who would dare call themselves an astrologist would be on a quest of improving the image of the study and give a care about being true to the discipline.

Those whose intentions are only to profit from the desperation of people would not even be worried about these important factors but would mask their greed for money and their want for recognition with flowery words and empty promises - so long as you click and buy, as soon as they get your payment details, and as soon as the cash gets to them. Yes, sadly the internet is rife with hordes of fakes. Some obvious traits are more blatant than others.

Word of mouth is always a good way to find a good and upstanding astrologist whose aim is to help improve a person's quality of life and to enlighten those who are open to the principles of both the art and the science of the discipline. Ultimately not everyone will understand the fundamentals of astrology but those gifted and skilled with the patience will press on to discover the many wonders of the mathematical science and genius of the discipline. They would have a good reputation amongst their peers and well as with clients. They would be glad to share time with you and have you consult with them even after the fact. These are the sort of astrologers you want to deal with.

You will find many reputable astrologers online who have uploaded videos of themselves talking about astrology and how it works. This is a convenient way of checking them out visually since you will be able to size up their intentions. Knowing if they have actual skills, well, only you can tell after. There are a number of astrologers who have uploaded videos of themselves giving free lessons which you can access anytime, without having to pay them a penny for their lessons. But if you want a more hands on, comprehensive, personal experience of a natal reading, you can also take advantage of seeing them at work and decide whether they are worth getting in touch with.

One of the more "screaming fake and generated" website scams is email spamming. Individuals with one name, just one name, would profess to be the know all and be all of all things and will entice you with sweet words, like "my dearest, I know how devastated you feel…" or "I see that you have been struggling financially for so long but I see I large amount of money coming your way…" or something along those lines, and would typically sign off their long ass letter with a single name. Keep away from them.

A self-respecting astrologer will not have any problems giving you their name nor would they have any qualms meeting up with you personally, if feasible geographically. They ideally should and must give you an hour to an hour and a half of their time after you have gone over and reviewed your astrological chart and be ready with upfront answers to your pressing questions. Another would boast of being "Astrologers to the Stars" but in fact is just a catchy banner sign garishly boasting an untruth.

Upstanding ones will charge you a fee just as charlatans would. Most certified astrologers would charge anywhere from $100-$250. These charts take a little while to figure out and put together and decipher, is why. Whereas frauds would probably charge you anywhere in the mid-range of those prices but upsell the rest of "your chart and readings" for an astronomically ridiculous price with no thought of you. They latch on to you by enticing you with promises of revealing even more "shocking revelations" that you "will discover IF you buy" the rest of the reading.

If their website has a turnaround period of 30 minutes to an hour, you should be warned that you are reading is more likely a computer generated piece of crap that touches on vague generalizations or outright balderdash that'll have you scratching your head in vain. Hence the scam begins.

Chapter Three: Astrology: A Millennia of Studies and Beyond

Surpassing time the study of astrology may have been frowned or laughed upon then and now, but there is undoubtedly numerous evidence showing the prevalence of the discipline being alive and well and still a subject of interest in our present century, whether they be believers in the science and art of the discipline or naysayers and skeptics the study of the alignment of planets and stars along with the sun and the moon has fascinated many as much as provoked them. It is a highly charged subject of debate and wonder amongst many.

See for yourself and find out how astrology factored into the daily lives of historical personas and you will understand why it is what it is. Understand the bearing of what happens above in the heavens in relation to the events we experience here on earth.

Perhaps it is because in our core of cores we aim to strive to come to know better our higher selves. Astrology is aimed to put us on a higher plane of self-realization, self-awareness, self-exploration, and self-explanation. Other branches of astrology are still widely used to this day and should also be worth your while to know about more. The many facets of how this ancient study of the planetary bodies has influenced the daily lives of many, and the many who attest by it, bear witness as to why astrology still holds its own weight in modern society even in the face of fast moving technology.

Given the weight it has on many, astrology continues to give credence to the fact that we cannot help but look up to the night sky, as if in prayer, in search for clues.

Ancient Astrology

Many great men like Copernicus Galileo, Ptolemy, and Aristotle were some of the early astrologers who stirred in the minds of many other thinkers what the stars and planets may hold and what they tell us. These celestial shifts and movements fascinated others after them to ask more questions about what is beyond our planet so much so that astronomy was once a subject of science. The many suppositions of these great thinkers would eventually pave the way for people to use their imaginings in a way that would allow us to contradict, answer, give solutions and reveal information.

They were not the only ones who had great ideas about the universe and the planets and stars it holds but It was them and others like them who stirred the minds of many other intellectuals throughout time, time and again, to challenge or solidify their initial ideas. Astrology, in a grand gesture of providing knowledge of what is seen in the heavens, allowed the expansion of the study of the universe, man, and his being, as well as other disciplines of science that give us the luxuries and technologies we enjoy today. Many of what were once imagined and fathomed only in the recesses of the mind of man, are now realities in our lives. What once was thought to be only possible in fantasy has become a reality because of the initial work and documentation of sky observers of the past.

But it was also because of those advancements that gave way to bigger questions about the reality and accuracy of what astrology claims to bring to the table. And because it has been so widely misunderstood for what it stands and what it imparts, it had lost its luster and dulled the interests of many when claims relating to and about astrology were made. However, there was always a small minority of individuals who continued to study astrology and adjusted their perceptions to open up a wider more expansive knowledge of it.

The mathematical aspect of this science was dug into deeper and secretly studied by many when others were persecuted, imprisoned and others even put to death because of the information they shared - sometimes a complete false, other times accurate, while there are theories earlier refuted but later (much later) was proven to be true.

Astrology is a set of principles that if followed, practiced, conveyed and understood correctly, tells us of our place under the sun and essentially helps us explain situations and events in our lives. It does not take away free will from us nor does invoke to have an individual believe that they have no choice and "it is written in the stars". Astrology aims to further the knowledge of oneself with one's own using the knowledge man has gained according to the planets and stars pull on our inner being. It aims to shed light on you, as an individual A guide, if you may, to assist you at any given time of your life.

Modern Astrology

The fast movement of scientific knowledge recently has seen great advancement in terms of machinery and tools that allows us the modern conveniences we have that many of us take for granted. Many of these inventions and tools of the many branches of the sciences are greatly owed to many individuals of long bygone history whose imaginings went far beyond their space and realm of time. Because of all these we are now able to enjoy many perks and advantages not available to those who came before us.

Astrology may have waned in the interest and curiosity of people by the 17th century but had picked up interest anew when the 1970's rolled around. There are presently a few schools around the world that teach Astrology to students curious about the craft and discipline of the study. To further the institution of astrology, schools have not only streamlined the practice, but have also gone so far as to certify individuals who have passed the standards founded on the study. The advent of these formal schools and eventual certification gives credence to the fact that astrology is and will be a system of looking at their circumstances, events and situations from a higher perspective, if you must.

Today's technology has contributed to the clarity of what astronomy is and has given astrologers a better perception of the relation of planets and stars to the daily events and circumstances of individuals. Because of the great advancement of our knowledge about the universe, the discovery of "new" planets has allowed astrology to compartmentalize and able to generalize readings, i.e. when is the best date and times to officially open that coffee and pastry shop you've always wanted.

Back then an astrologer's job was a tedious one of creating a chart - and you shall have a good idea of the time spent on this as we shall go over making one later in the book. A chart takes precision and mathematical calculations in order to get all the quantifiers in alignment. It took a lot of sheets of paper, elbow grease, and mindful thought to measurements to come up with an accurate chart. Nowadays, technological modernity has allowed

Computers, and computer software has allowed astrologers the convenience of having a software create a chart based on information given by an individual, but it would still take a practicing or seasoned astrologer to read those charts and interpret them using the methods and applying the principles of the discipline they have learnt. This is where the human touch remains. Here is when the astrologer is present for any questions an individual may have. Here is where the astrologer can tell you what you can't decipher for yourself.

Chapter Four: So, you want to become an astrologer?

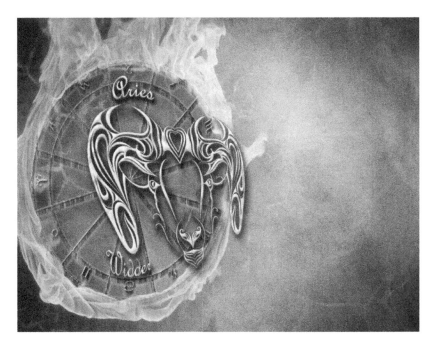

If you are reading this in the hopes of studying the craft and science of astrology, then you have picked up the right book. If it is your curiosity about the subject matter and knowing more about astrology is what compelled you to pick up this book, then you have made the right choice as well. You will not only find out about the workings of astrology, its history and the aim of the discipline, you will also get to know a little better as you discover the signs in the heavens and their significance to you.

Whether you are looking to start with your own chart, or have been self-teaching yourself with bits and pieces of the discipline which you have picked up here and there, from short articles on the internet or if it is for a higher purpose, what you are reading now is geared toward your overall enlightenment on all of the aspects that come along with learning and fine-tuning this ancient science and skill. It is also geared toward self-enlightenment and awareness.

With any endeavor close to your heart, approach it with gusto and fervor and passion. The little times when we can be in control of something (free will, remember?) you need to want it bad enough that you work toward it. "Plans are made is too broken" - or so a twisted saying goes...It is not enough that you make a plan. In reality, solutions do not come out of plans but they are the results of the plans we execute. Plans we test and carry out.

In other words, plan out your schedule and see what works for you. You will need to put in a chunk of your time into studying if you intend to learn well. Choose which methods of learning you want. Do you want to apprentice for someone else more experienced? This will cost you time and possibly at the beginning small to no income. Plan anyway.

Would you rather learn online? What are the best online schools? Are they credible? What ratings and user experience remarks do they have on their page? Are they certified? Will they be able to certify you? What sort of certification is it? There are beginners, advanced and crash courses available online; how long is it? How much is it? Just some questions to start you off on your quest to looking for one online, if off-site learning is best for your time. Plan anyway.

A friend of mine from France studied astrology, in an actual class in an actual building, after office hours. She was tickled pink to find out that she could finally take up astrology subsidized by her company and the government, because it had long fascinated her. She had even made me one of her practice reads. She is still practicing her skills during off-work hours saying it is also a hobby of hers so it doesn't impede on her life or finances. Just keep planning and practicing anyway!

Chapter Five: The Study of Astrology

Imbibe the spirit of wanting to be true to the craft and the discipline. Change the wrong and very sketchy impression a truckload of self-serving individuals caused by their grubby wiles. Live true to its truths, like the math involved in the study and the disciple's limitations (Can't give you the winning lotto numbers. Remember?), and have it find its respectful spot back in society and history.

How to Be a Proficient Astrologer

All good outcomes take time, effort and patience. Being a good astrologer will mean that you have to put in your time and, as with any new study you take up anything new you want to learn, have the patience with yourself. Think about your end goal and what it is you purpose to do with the skill once you graduate. Sometimes we are started off driven by mere passion and only later on find specific reasons answering the why's and the what's.

Why is it important to know this early on? Well, first of all you will need to plan out your time. You will need to figure out your finances. If you have no background or experience in the subject but only want to dabble in the basics then you will probably not be able go as far as doing readings for other people and get paid for services rendered. If that is the case then you will probably only be dealing with skimming over a vaster study.

But there are many classifications of the discipline of astrology from business astrology, to medical astrology and these are two categories studied and practiced for reasons relating to finances and health. There are others that focus just on creating and reading natal charts and those that focus on the generalities and base their calculations on the sun sign of a person. Again these will be things you will want to determine and find out as you go deeper into finding out about the many branches of astrology.

The advances we have made in technology is perhaps one of the reasons why Astrology has become more and more visible in the mainstream arena of our technologically advanced world. Computer applications are now better able to help the potential astrologer into figuring out past planetary placements in the sky (which once upon a time was a very useful tool for weather pattern predictions).

Astrology - What's In It For Me?

The beauty about having and meeting goals is that these goals pave the way for new things you want to achieve and fresh ideas you want to test. End goals are not really the end but only the start to new beginnings. You may be here, reading this book right now thinking about learning the craft a wee bit more for personal purposes, like reading your own natal chart or for fun like reading natal charts for your friends. Plain curiosity. Perhaps you feel it's a gift, a calling if you may that propelled you here. Or this may well be something you take to heart and want to share with the rest of humanity - or at least those who want to be reached. Those reasons may change and they may not.

In other words you may start out on the path of learning, entering with one reason in mind but could come out with new knowledge about why you felt compelled to know more about this ancient craft and mathematical logic of astrology. There is so much to discover about it and in turn, yourself.

What Astrology Tells Us

Astrology allows us to explain ourselves and where we are in the larger scheme of the picture. Sure that could include the general future too, but as with anything we do in our lives, different paths could lead to a different direction. Or it could lead us around in circles. This is where astrology can give us foresight into what decisions to make at certain events or situations we may later find ourselves. If we haven't said it enough, let us say it again - Astrology is not a tool to predict future events nor can it be relied on to "see" and get privy to events unknown to us.

It is a tool that, if used wisely, will allow us to explain our place in this world. It is a tool that allows us to see into what traits we possess that we may not have tapped into yet. It gives us insight on ourselves and tells us of the limitations we have - not to make concrete our belief that are not adept to do one thing or another, what it intends is to help us see those weaknesses and give us a better understanding of ourselves, making us stronger and easily adaptable to change and shift. In other words, it reveals what areas in our lives we can work on to strengthen or inhibit some traits.

This is why we are given the strengths and weaknesses of each zodiac. To tell us where we can excel and what areas we need to develop and strengthen.

For the generalizations like, businesses and financial ventures, it gives us the best possible times of planetary or star alignments which show better favor. This practice is still widely used by many counter-parts like, Vietnam, China, Laos, Thailand for their reference and strongly adhere to the principles of astrology to determine the best time to start on a business venture i.e. partnering up with another person (are you compatible and do you complement each other?), opening a business establishment (when is the best time to open up a store that would allow the business to get a good foothold?), and so forth. In the end it is these general details which allow us to make better decisions about things that we do on a day to day basis.

There are other facets of astrology which delves into the medical and financial aspects of everyday life. There are also categories of astrology which is practiced for weather pattern and events, politics, and starting a new employment. The one which is most known is the natal astrology, and possibly one that a novice would start with in terms of deeper understanding and studies of the discipline, which is based on the place of birth and time of birth of an individual. This is what we shall be looking into more as we go over the next chapters of this book.

Chapter Six: The Basics of Astrology

Let's dig a little deeper and get to know the basics of what there is to know on creating a birth chart. It is a time sensitive, data based chart consisting of one of the Four Elements (fire, water, earth and air) combined with either one of Three Qualities which could either be the Fixed, the Cardinal or the Mutable quality, this shows us the connection between all things breathing and have matter on this Earth and how we are tied in together in the bigger picture. It shows us that we are part of a cycle.

It is not to say that this is the end all and be all of your persona, personality or being. There are good and a bad characteristic that you will see on each of the four elements but it does not describe you in completion. What Astrology is an outline, if you must, of your capabilities, potential and weaknesses and how you the study can you recognize some of these traits and evolve. It essentially helps you learn more about yourself and what you can do to either overcome or enhance in your life.

These are the basic precepts you will need to know in order to be able to make calculated decisions about any given event at any given time of your life. In this chapter we will go over the foundation of astrology and learn about the signs, planetary houses, the role of the sun and the moon to us.

Discover your own sign to be privy to your weaknesses - so as to be able to make adjustments and realize your "limitations" and be empowered to overcome your own fears which you feel may be holding you back. Confirm your strengths and gain the knowledge of your sleeping self and allow these traits innate to you be awakened to help enhance your life and being. Have a deeper sense of perception of yourself and get a clearer picture of what you are to help you get to where you want to be.

In the end we are given free will and the choice is for us to make on which of these traits, negative or positive alike, we will build up or tone down. The essence in fact is not to put down the individual but help the individual realize these elemental powers and how we can use them for good and how we can transform and evolve from the negative aspects into a more near-perfect being.

Join us for a brief look into the celestial bodies that we look upon to give us clearer insight of our being and let's discover what they each mean and how looking up allows us a better understanding of events in our lives but more importantly - a look into ourselves.

The Four Elements of Western Astrology

The traditional Chinese, Vietnamese, Japanese and Bon and Hindu Astrology deals with Five elements namely; Fire, Air, Water, Earth and Void whereas Western Astrology follows the four classical elements of Fire, Water, Earth, and Air. We shall be looking deeper into the Four Elements and Three Qualities applied by Western Astrology in this chapters as well as the next chapters following after this.

The creative and electrical are the markers of the Fire element; Earth, with its binding properties, tie in the other three elements allowing the formation of matter using the other element properties; Air, allows for a sort of detachment of the main elements of Water and Fire, allowing co-existence; and Water, the element possessing magnetic qualities which sustain us and nurture us are the classical elements which explain the intricacies of all matter and each of our individualities in simpler terms.

The diversities of the world we exist in are boundless and this goes to say too for our individualities. These four elements make up a sign's personality traits; i.e. strengths and weaknesses. Each of the houses represents various areas of being wherein the planets and horoscope signs work. We shall be looking at which sign falls under which element one by one in a bit but indulge as we describe the workings of the four elements in a simplified manner.

To simplify things a little, imagine a tree. We all know that the roots of the tree are what absorb the water from the earth - let that be the analogy for the 2 elements of Earth and Water. These two elements marry in harmony and gives life. The leaves are basically the lungs of the tree allowing the tree to breathe and it also absorb the nutrients of the sun through those leaves allowing a cycle of being - let this be the analogy of Air. These two elements sustain life.

Take a log of the tree and set it on fire and the water in it evaporates into the air. The sunlight which shone on the tree would be emitted as flames and the oxygen it releases allows the log and the soil to turn to ash, which will serve as a nutritional source for other forms of life, making another complete cycle.

Human beings have all these four elements as well. If this delicate balance were disrupted in a person it would pave the way for disease and the blockage of energies. Stunting and depriving oneself of these energies are also sometimes unconscious things we do to ourselves. Too much of anything which inhibits other elements is always a probable situation in the life of a human being. Not only would your doctor advise against it but your body on its own gives it telltale signs and warnings, which you should well heed, when you overdo things.

The Four Elements and What They Mean

Each of these elements is neither good nor bad but neutral. It is the individual who inherently gives way to disrupting the harmony and balance of the elements and man who develops in himself the good and bad traits. So this is exactly why we are looking into the strengths of each individual sign and element - it is not to make you feel less than you are but to have you understand that and make the necessary adjustments, and to understand that we do have limitations and some of those limitations are things we can overcome.

The signs falling under Fire are known as extroverts or are also called the masculine traits. Water and Earth signs are more feminine in qualities and sometimes referred to as negative traits.

Some of the positive qualities of the signs which fall under the Fire element include their enthusiasm and vigor. They are a courageous bunch with zeal. This element delivers creativity and they are known for being brave. On the other hand, the not-so-positive qualities of the signs classified under the Fire element include tendency to excess, jealousy, violence, anger, hate. They tend to destroy and are vindictive; they get easily irritated and are quite quarrelsome. They are voracious and lean toward violence. Some of the signs which are categorized under the Fire Elements are Leo, Aries and Sagittarius.

The positive qualities of the Air element includes being mild in manner, and watchful. They display and a trusting nature, they are known for being kind hearted and devoted. They display clarity, dexterity and are optimists. Those who fall under this element are independent, as well as diligent. They are a pretty joyful bunch. On the other hand the negative traits of those who fall under the Air element is their tendency to gossip. Signs under this element can be quite cunning. They can be quite sensitive and touchy. They can also be inconsistent, with a lack of perseverance and dishonest. Libra, Aquarius and Gemini are the signs which fall under the Air Element.

Earth, is a female or introvert element and the signs of Virgo, Taurus and Capricorn fall under this category. The signs that fall under this element are known for being persevering. Signs under this element are also known for their consistency, mindfulness, ambition, and straight-forwardness. They are responsible and steadfast known for punctuality and reliability. On the other hand the negative traits of signs under this element show that they lack consciousness, and scorn. They can be quite timid and cumbersome, known also to be lazy, indifferent and superficial.

Some of the stronger traits of those who fall under the element of Water are that they are a trusting bunch by nature; they are placid, understanding, and mild in manner. They are a forgiving lot who are compassionate who are devoted. They like to internalize and enjoy the company of their thoughts as they are meditative. Those signs falling under the Water Element category are modest and do things with fervor. On the other hand they can be quite indifferent and heartless with circumstances and situations they may find unsavory. They aren't exactly the most daring bunch, and tend to be a tad lazy. They tend to display dejection, can be pretty unstable and tend to display lack of concern and instability. Cancer, Pisces and Scorpio are signs which fall under the category of the Water Element.

Chapter Seven: The 12 Houses of the Zodiac

    In the pursuit of delving deeper into the meanings of all the components that make up a birth chart, we shall divide the twelve Houses, into two parts according to the Elements they fall under. Information about these Houses pertains to the fields of experience and not necessarily on individual or actual experiences. This chapter, and the next one, will hopefully allow you a comprehensive and clearer picture of each of the individual traits of each House and how it ties in with anyone (or two or three) of the Four Elements and the three Qualities discussed earlier.

The 12 Houses is based on the 24 hour rotation of the Earth whereas the Zodiac signs are based on the Sun's orbit annually around our planet.

The astrological natal chart shows twelve segments and is what the House is composed of is each ruled by a Zodiac sign. An astrologer would read the houses counterclockwise on a natal chart combining the meaning of each wanderer (planet) with consideration to the house the planet (wanderer) is in as well as the zodiac sign (the outer wheel) under which it falls - essentially providing the individual with a map of talents and challenges which the individual will encounter during this lifetime. Every house has a set of characteristics and begins with the individual and the chart expands and reaches the throes of society and farther.

The wanderers or the planets were all set under houses and signs at the time of an individual's birth into this earth. This chapter, we shall be discussing the personal houses which are the twelve houses of Aries, Taurus, Gemini, Cancer, Leo, Virgo, Libra, Scorpio, Sagittarius, Pisces, Capricorn, Aquarius,

The 12 Houses of the Zodiac

The House of Aries

The First House is Aries and is ruled by the planet Mars. It is a Masculine sign and is the first fire sign and the first cardinal sign of the houses. Aries rules over the head. The birthstone of Aries is the heliotrope and they are energetic beings who are set on courage and truth.

The House of Taurus

The Second House is Taurus and it is a Feminine sign. It is the first Earth sign as well as the first fixed sign. This House is ruled by Venus. Taurus resides in the throat and neck. The birthstone of Taurus is emerald and they make great cooks, artist and entertainers. They are tranquil and sensual. They are known to be simple and quiet in nature and non-competitive.

The House of Gemini

The third House is where Gemini lies. Gemini lords over all kinds of communication forms. This house also is relative to siblings, schools, bibliotheques, community affairs, local travel and neighborhoods. Gemini is governed by Mercury as the lungs, thorax and arms. The birthstone of Gemini is crystal and they make great journalists, teachers, salespeople, hosts and presenters.

The House of Cancer

At the bottom of the wheel is the fourth house where sits Cancer. This is the fourth zodiac and since it sits at the bottom of the zodiac wheel it is regarded as the foundation of everything, inclusive of the need for privacy, the need for basic security. The House of Cancer deals with mothering traits of nurturing. The birthstone of Cancer is the moonstone. They are perfect for dealing with antiquities, are good archeologists, suitable in the catering or hotel business.

The House of Leo

The fifth House is Leo and governs the eyes, spine, and the heart. It is the second fire sign and is a fixed sign ruled over by the Sun. It governs creativeness in the individual as it rules over self-expression, attention as well as play and recreational fun. It is a Masculine sign. Its birthstone is the diamond.

The House of Virgo

The sixth House, Virgo is where service and wellness of health resides and is ruled by Mercury. Virgo is related to the intestines. It lords over routines, diet and exercising, healthy living the natural and simple way. They are in-service to others and are good in ruling schedules and have good organizational skills. Their birthstone is agate and they make very good medical practitioners i.e. doctors, paramedics, nurses, caregivers, etc. It involves the manner of how we work and respond to everyday things and issues.

The House of Libra

The seventh House is Libra. It is governed by Venus and relates to how we respond to our life relationships. It is the house which lords over the personally binding relationships and business partnerships which come with a contract in shared-relations involving enemies, marriage, divorce, fights, and lawsuits. It is the second Air sign and the third Cardinal sign of Masculinity. Its birthstone is opal. Those falling under this House are creators of artistic proportions, who hold jobs in the luxury, beauty or fashion industry. They could be musicians, excellent lawyers and great mediators. House is ruled over by Venus is the second Air sign as well as the third Cardinal sign that is Masculine. It represents what we are with regard to relations with other people and rules over personal and enterprise partnerships. It lords over associations of relations which involve contracts like business deals, business contracts and marriage.

The House of Scorpio

The Eighth House is Scorpio. It is the second water sign and the third fixed sign with Mars ruling. It is the house that lords over changes and is mysterious as this is the house where birth, death, joint forces, sex and bonding at its deepest level. It rules over monies and possessions i.e. property, investments and inheritance. Their birthstone is malachite and they can be gynecologists and psychiatrists, guardians of the law like military or police. They are also good stock brokers and managers of assets. They are known for their aggressive nature which can be impulsive aiding the change of any event they are dealing with. They get to know others with their nature of being upfront not because they aim to hurt but because they aim to get to know another individual better by their reaction.

The House of Sagittarius

The Ninth House is Sagittarius whose nature is to see everything traveling far distances, aim for higher learning and foreign languages. They are known for their optimism.

The House of Pisces

Pisceans are inspirational individuals that tend to be good in higher learning. They gain knowledge through learning and are driven by their ethics and morality. The tenth House is ruled over by Jupiter and is the third fire sign which is masculine and mutable.

The House of Capricorn

The eleventh House, Capricorn is governed by Saturn and is the third Earth sign which is Feminine. It is also the fourth Cardinal sign governing over the bones, skin and knees. The birthstone of those under the sign of Capricorn is jade, and they are phlegmatic in the image they portray themselves. They seem reserved as they ponder on decisions and are careful to respond, mindful of the environment around them.

The House of Aquarius

The twelfth House is ruled over by Aquarius and is the third Earth sign of Masculinity. It is also the fourth fixed sign of the zodiac. Their birthstone is sapphire and they make good astrologers, physicists, actors and scientists. They are suited for projects aiming for the betterment of their communities.

The Twelfth House is ruled by Neptune and Jupiter and is the fourth Mutable sign which is Feminine. Pisces governs over blood, its circulation as well as the feet. Their profession takes them off to sea and long trips on through air, land and seas. Their birthstone is amethyst and they also make great doctors, writers and best suited to work in far off places from their homestead.

You may have come to notice, or soon enough will, that the rank of the Houses lead to the path of an individual's developmental life. This commences o the first house or the impulse of the person. You will see a pattern form and come to understand that each of the Houses represent the generalities of each.

The planets housed in the angular houses are the most influential ones and the most important ones as well. The first, fourth, seventh and tenth houses are the most vital Houses they coincide with the four angles of the ascendant, I.C., descendant and M.C.

Discover what influences you and where you are in the bigger picture of not only this world but how your fate is mirrored in the celestial bodies of the heavens.

Chapter Eight: Zodiac Signs and What They Mean

In this chapter, you'll learn the meaning and significance of each signs or houses in the Zodiac. This is the general meanings and interpretations of each sign, and it's only created for the purposes of showing the general references or guidelines for each. The meanings can change depending on the situations, seasons, and other specificity. Use the information found in this chapter as your main guideline in drawing out conclusions or interpretations when doing a reading to your subject.

Aries

The first sign which fall under the zodiac of Aries are best suited to become surgeons, law officers, entrepreneurs and athletes. The favored day of Aries is Tuesday and the color of this sign is red. The birthstone of Aries is the heliotrope. The Arian displays authority and may sometimes come off and be misunderstood as arrogant. They are energetic in a very efficient and straightforward manner. They have a tendency to be headstrong and go for their goals with great gusto which can in turn cause them harm. Their positive traits of enthusiasm, courage, straightforwardness may come off and be displayed as aggression, rebelliousness and vulnerability.

Taurus

The signs and the Ascendant which fall under the second zodiac of Taurus are singers, artists; they are excellent in the kitchen. They are good bankers and estate realtors. They are patient, loyal, steady and consistent. They are tough and persevering. They are strong and focus as they are stable and concrete. They are tenacious and robust. They are faithful. Taurus enjoys life and tranquility. As much as sensuality is on top of the Taurus' life they are also naturally reserved and like living a simple life. Not being competitive in spirit makes the Taurean a happy individual with a calm demeanor. They have practice common sense which leads them to feel fulfilled and are not questers to vie for first place. They exert sustainable energy and making things is important to this sign. They are gentle, and process ideas and thoughts carefully and mindfully. Once they make up their minds, it is set. They are not one for change and do not adapt quickly to it.

Gemini

The third zodiac is Gemini. The Gemini mind hops from one idea to another as quick as can be, spending a great deal of time asking and seeking answers to questions. The Gemini mind is constantly churning and working as they come up with solutions to problems and challenges and is able to back these up with knowledge they learn quickly. They are movers and shakers who seem to be everywhere at once. The Gemini is expressively sociable, clever, quick-witted and funny. They are intelligent, adaptable and lively. They are imaginatively creative and fanciful. On the other hand they are also the moody ones, who can be shallow at times. They ask a lot of questions therefore are inquisitive. They are also known to be capricious and opportunistic, unfazed and selfish.

Cancer

The fourth zodiac of Cancer is said to be oriented and driven to nostalgia for things bygone. They deeply rooted and instinctively protect themselves from the world around them with an inner life enviably rich with a clear and vivid imagination making sure to avoid risks pursuant toward security. They are only comfortable in letting down their guard around people they know they can trust. They find solace and comfort in reminiscing about past events. They are sentimental and emotional. They are the sensitive and imaginative sort who are protective of their family especially mother and and children. They are poetic, tender and nurturing individuals. On the other hand they also tend to be greedy as they are generous. They can be moody and stubborn as they can be lazy. They can also be inaccessible and lazy.

Leo

The fifth zodiac is Leo and individuals falling under this zodiac are powerful forces of self-confidence. Leo is psychologically inclined by nature who is a good leader with stability and nobility when in command. Leo commands the respect of people who surround them. The charisma they possess puts them under the limelight because of their ability to put things in order and command respect. They are a determined bunch who is strong-willed, loyal and courageous. Leo is creative, a fighter who likes to win, they are fiery and happy people. They are seductive and daring, responsible and honest. The individuals who fall under the zodiac of Leo are on the other hand vain, mulish, impatient, and quick to get angry or lose patience, they are intolerant and self-centered.

Virgo

The sixth zodiac is Virgo with traits attributed to a psychological nature who likes to proceed with caution. The Virgo individual likes to mull things over and turn it around in their head looking at a situation from all aspects and perspectives as they imagine reactions and results. They strive to come up with the answers closest to what is considered to be the best possible answers to a problem presented to them. They are problem solvers who are perfectionists and who will not stop until they have the best and closest to optimally resolve situational problems. They are not exactly spontaneous individuals therefore they can sometimes miss out on enjoying life to its fullest. Their being guarded prevents them from experiencing life at its fullest.

Libra

The seventh zodiac is Libra and is ruled over by both Venus whose qualities display as attractiveness, extraversion, balance, and harmony or by Saturn whose nature is restrained, introverted, and meditative. Libra's nature depends on who governs the strongest. When Saturn is at work on the chart of a person falling under the sign of Libra, the Libran is fragile, outgoing, ever compromising and delicate. This is the reason why some who fall under this zodiac is deemed weak or unwilling to commit to sharing an opinion or voicing out their thought, preferring instead to act as the pacifier and unifying situations with harmony and understanding however it may take away from their being assertive.

Libras despise violence and adjust to events and situations gracefully. They are elegant, indulgent, ethereal, loyal, and sentimental. Those under the zodiac of Libra are polite and refined, seductive and considerate as well as indulgent of things they deem beautiful, enticing, engaging. They are indecisive, fearful and can be weak, insensitive and cold.

Scorpio

The eighth zodiac is Scorpio known for their rebellion and aggressive attitude. Ruled by Mars and governing the rectum and the genital and the sexual regions. They are both magnetic and charismatic. Scorpios are strong-willed and domineering as they are powerful and secretive. Those under this sign are passionate and independent. Known for their creativity and cunning they are also ambitious and competitive. They are proud, untamable and sexual. They are stubbornly aggressive in nature and can be prone to destruction. They can get violent and destructive. This zodiac is complex in their love for themselves as they are jealous.

Sagittarius

Sagittarius is the ninth zodiac and is a masculine sign whose naturally independent and outgoing. The Sagittarian in geared toward being energetically active possessing the soul of a leader who is likeable. They are the tidy ones who are amusing yet straightforward. They are charming and adventurous as well as exuberant and making them great people to put in positions of leadership. The mind of a Sagittarius is always aimed higher and farther and is known to love liberty exuberantly.

Capricorn

The tenth zodiac is that of Capricorn who nature is utter control and introverted. They are seen as austere when in fact they are positioning and steeling themselves in the environment they face. They are steadfast and reliable and are suited to be put in long-term service. They are more averse to working on their spiritual self and value rather than get tied down by materialistic riches. They are known for being cautious and thoughtful as they are lucid. Sagittarians are hard-working and possess strong-will as well as recognition of responsibility. They are the ones who driven by perseverance and are patient as they wait. Those under this sign are realistic individuals who are resolute and moralists. On the other hand they can be also curt, petty, selfish, skeptical and dull.

Aquarius

Aquarius is the eleventh zodiac whose traits include altruism, independence and detachment. They are surprising individuals who possess creative skills and are tolerant, generous beings they fancy themselves to be originals but are modest and reserved. They value friendships and see themselves as links to friendly relations making good community members and leaders as they lead and pave and set examples of charitable deeds and neighborly generosity. They can also be cold and different from the "norm". They may display resignation to situations uncontrolled by them and show to have difficulty in being adjusted to changes.

Pisces

The twelfth and final zodiac, Pisces rules over endings. By nature they are easily adaptable, imaginative individuals who are flexible. They are emotionally sensitive and compassionate as they are romantic and nice. They grab opportunities they see with fervor and are intuitive individuals who are charming introverts. On the other hand they can come off as moody, dreamers whose thoughts are everywhere all at once. It is difficult for the gullible Piscean to be placed under any category as they are supremely ruled over by their emotions.

Many consider the twelfth zodiac to be humanity's collective unconscious. Pisceans are dedicated individuals who are adaptable to changes in their environment. They are sensitive and are driven with emotions rather than reason and intellect. They are the intuitive ones who are rather introverted and tend toward secrecy. They are the artistically charming lot who are difficult to classify. They are compassionate as they are wild. They are the romantics.

Chapter Nine: The Moon and the Zodiac Signs

Let's take a closer look at the celestial body nearest to us, the Moon. The moon has been the topic of many stories from the past. It has been spoken about and written into literature, philosophy, epochs, poetry, science, and pop culture. The Moon is a key player in the grand scheme of things with regard to our daily lives and the whimsical, spontaneous decisions we make. There is no good and bad in the sign of the moon itself it is essentially the choices we make which affect or effect a situation later on.

The Moon in Relation to the Zodiac Signs

The Moon is what drives the instinctive habits in us to go off like clockwork and it is the moon which creates the reactions we unconsciously make. Finding your place under the Sun and getting to know more about your sign under the Moon gives more revelatory information about our inner self and workings. Things deep down inside us that even we may not be aware of or realize! Whereas the Sun is logical in its movements so is the Moon reactively illogical to the actions of the Sun.

Ever wonder how you respond to challenges the way you do in hindsight? Wonder how you can curb unsavory reactions to situations and events around you that you may not find favorable? Look to the Moon which is associated with feminine qualities of nurturing, responsiveness and of internal reflection. It is both your inner maternal instinct and your inner child all rolled into one. How the Moon orbits around the Sun is a reflection of the protective nature it possesses. A protective nature we dig deep into when we are looking for solace, comfort, safety and security.

It is what gives us spirit and gives spring to our steps as it rules the ins and outs of active energies that flow and come from within ourselves. The Moon acts as the go-between and mediates the inner and outer worlds of the signs. It rules the tropic of Cancer working in the capacity of our inner private desires and our unconscious thoughts and inner self-dialogs. The aim of astrology is also to help a person reveal their higher self and overcome inherent traits which may be derailing them.

Some signs are driven more by the Moon than the Sun. Particularly so for signs falling under a water sign like Cancer, Pisces and Scorpio or a united angle near the corner of 4th or 10th House. Find the balance in your Moon sign to obtain true joy in your heart.

Since the Moon moves and appears to us on Earth differently every 2-3 days, it is important for you to determine yours. Your Moon sign is about the deepest part of yourself. It is the architect of your inner self. Your emotions, your desires, your needs, your wants, your imaginings, your thoughts, your wishes, it is what gives vibrancy to underlying feelings and emotions you experience. It is where strength is drawn from to attain a certain sense of emotional security.

Discovering your Moon sign is also interesting to know because it could be influencing traits in you which are otherwise not necessarily present in your House or Zodiac sign. Ever wonder why a natal reading trait just does not seem to fit what you know about yourself? Well, don't forget the Moon factor that strongly influences the lives we live internally. An intense Aries combined with the mellow Moon of a Taurean could ease your innate aggressive nature. Now isn't that a far cry from just reading your natal birth chart without paying a bit of mind to your Moon! Shall we delve in deeper and discover your Moon under your sign? Discover the traits within you.

THE MOON IN ARIES

Let's begin with the obvious beginning, Aries. The Moon over Aries is passionate on, with the need to blaze on as it contemplates, searches, and experiments to gain results. The quicker the better! Feelings are cast aside and activity and movement masks having to deal with sentiments anew to them. The Moon over Aries is one with a temper. Unpredictable and volatile unlike a Piscean who would retreat into themselves when on a low streak of self-confidence hits them.

A person under this sign is undoubtedly independent and is not afraid to take chances. The people with Moon in Aries are an easily bored bunch and looks for more exciting environments when they start feeling antsy. They are the lord over the pride and you will be sure to have every interesting interaction with family members who fall under this position of the moon in Aries. When a Moon over Aries sets their sights on something they want they don't like to wait around and have fate work its wonder and allow whatever it is to fall in their laps. They are impulsive and have short-lived wants that taste so palpable to them at the time of thought that what was wanted becomes what is needed. Take a positive spin on this and you would notice that a moon in Aries do not like to have anything drag on; it will be clear what a Moon in Aries wants when they want it. The Moon in Aries individual, like a adorable child manages to charm their way into people's lives and have them run around looking for solutions.

THE MOON IN TAURUS

Having any sort of close relationship to a Moon in Taurus gives those closest to them a comfort in their steadiness. Intimacy and familiarity is vital to the strong-willed Moon Taurean. They are pretty steadfast in their manner and well rooted in what they have grown up to believe. They are not the sort to be pushed into anything they have not set out to do on their own, but once they make up their minds and set their heart to something, they persevere.

Lunar Taureans are not one for long, drawn out, sticky situations. They like things as predictable as can be and have a tendency to avoid any sort of emotional outbursts or crises that would rock their steady boat. They may not easily recognize a partners need to switch it up or feel that there is a lack in terms of emotional stimulation. However they do bask in building a solid homestead for themselves. Laying a strong foundation is important to keep the Lunar Taurean content.

The practicality of the Moon Taurean is so that they will hardly make a move on anything they sense won't add value to them or without making sure of the security of the situation. In general Moon Taureans are romantic with deep unwavering affections. They have strong but very meager needs; like what they would consider to be comfortable and familiar.

The practicality of this Earth sign and the position of the moon over it hint at their ability to secure themselves whilst keeping their interests well-guarded. These individuals are attuned to the physical world around the, and have a keen sense of smell. They are people who can be relied on for consistency who are loyal.

They thrive on routine and will hardly switch up habits for the heck of it. Since Taurus is a fixed sign people in relationships with a Taurean would understand how they would cling on to their partners however serious a conflict may be unraveling in their lives; breaking up is not something a Taurean would immediately consider in a tumultuous relationship. In fact, they bring a sort of calm to the table. Just don't disrupt their routine and habits as they are the least adaptable to sudden changes. They are not the spontaneous sort and are uncomfortable when something unexpected comes up. The Lunar Tauren thrives on their keen five senses and is important to them.

THE MOON IN GEMINI

Moon in Gemini are people who are curious about almost anything and have a great ability to gain and store information. They are great talkers, thinkers and readers. The Lunar Gemini is charming as they are clever and quick with a joke or a smart remark. Generally pleasant around people they tend to be a little shorter of temper when at home with their family. The moody Lunar Gemini generally does not like to do housework but love a good home improvement project which would keep them happy.

They are easily bored when things get too routine, habitual or predictably constant, frequently this is a reflection of their inner self and their hopes of greener pastures. Lunar Gemini's are open to varied ideas and have strong traits of being pliable and adaptable to changes. They love to switch things up to ward off boredom; they are the ones who take a different route to work routinely just to get out of the normalcy of the day. They are the best people to go to in terms of organizing big family shindigs as this takes the routine out of the normalcy of everyday routine. Lunar Gemini find it difficult to deal with other people's emotions something to remember when co - parenting with a Lunar Gemini. They are busy bees with a multitude of things on their plate that are intelligent, chatty and have a way with words.

They are a friendly bunch and is often in their best element seen socializing at large gatherings or events; a real life of the party, the Lunar Gemini is. And because of their savvy with language and words they like to hash things out by talking when problems loom. Watch out though for the Lunar Gemini tongue when they get irritated because they will snap at you. They are complicated when in a funk of a mood because it could signal inner turmoil which brings about the kind of moodiness that is complicated to decipher in a Moon Gemini.

THE MOON IN CANCER

Being the true governor of the sign, the Moon is most "comfortable" in Cancer. The Lunar Cancer is one who shows great promise in sensing and recognizing emotional changes people go through when they themselves are often wrapped up in their own world. They are reliable on remembering emotionally charged memories. The Moon in Cancer hang on to what they love is comfortable and familiar to them dearly. They love the feeling of being in familiar places, with familiar faces and hold fast to people they have deep connections with and are never out of sorts when this is their situation. They don't like change and find joy when things are quiet and peaceful.

Lunar Cancers loves a good laugh and has a great sense of humour and can leave you in stitches. They have a way of looking at things from a different perspective and possess a unique manner of looking at their lives. They can be irrational and find it difficult to detach one part of their lives with the rest of what goes on with them. To them everything is all and all is everything.

They have a tendency to hang on to past hurts and dwell on these hurts. They are great in getting another person's attention when they feel that they not given proper mind by a person they value. To make up for insecurities, Lunar Cancers could be averse to binge shopping or hoarding in order to curb feelings of insecurity. If provided with the security they so desire, when they feel understood and loved and cared for they are happy to return these feelings and share warmth.

It only takes a kind and thoughtful gesture to get them back in a good mood. In spite of the mood swings they possess Lunar Cancerians are highly dependable and reliable individuals, once you with their friendship you are a friend for life.

THE MOON IN LEO

One not to take orders rather is the one at the helm, the Lunar Leo likes to take control of things and take charge of their domain. They are the sort who require lots of affection and showered with tons of TLC to operate at an optimum level. They do not tend to be careful about their image in public hence they would never show if they are upset nor would they display grand gestures of displeasure. This changes when in their homestead, where they give in to emotional drama if they feel they have been slighted.

When comfortable around people the usually reserved Moon in Leo loved the sound of laughter. They are zany comics who are entertainers as well as they are creative. Lunar Leos have a desire for fairness, strong sense of justice and unwavering integrity. Don't spring a change of schedule with the stubborn Moon in Leo because they don't like that and actually need time to make inner adjustments because of their fairness you can be sure that you will not have to argue a point with them.

THE MOON IN VIRGO

We all need a Lunar Virgo in our lives. The one who never forgets to pay the bills and take care of the little things which turn out to be the mundane things we take for granted everyday but are important. The Moon in Virgo is the reliable one to count on to get the cash balancing of the household done, that eggs and milk are never for want and they do all of this with a skip in their steps but in secret. They would think they were unhappy about it because they'd be there right in your ear nagging you about one thing or another. They may complain quite a bit but show them a little appreciation, love and thought and they would be tickled pink to take care of you and the tiny the things that matter.

They are at their element when they feel productive and needed. They are the first in line to volunteer their services when something needs to get done. Needing to feel useful, the best scenario and day for a Moon In Virgo is when they are given a bunch of routine things to occupy their time with. They are happiest when they are going about carrying out routine tasks and mundane duties. They have the need to feel that they have made a contribution to getting the world in order, even if it is just the realm of space they move in, helping others in any way they can.

They are routine freaks whose day gets disrupted when their plans are waylaid. They get antsy and fidgety when things don't go according to plan. The Moon in Virgo needs routine and regularity to feel at ease and comfortable. They need to know that the little needful things have been done and that all is in order in their world. It is very difficult for a Moon in Virgo to see beyond the horizon. They know what their limits are and they are alright with that. They are definitely the ones to count on for the stuff that needs to get done every day. They are practical and give ready help and advice when they are turned to.

Lunar Virgos for lack of wanting to put themselves out there have been called unambitious and lacking in self-confidence but in fact this is what they know to be themselves and take pride in living simply and in the background giving support. They are the ones who worry too much and feel overwhelmed by anything that may cause stress or give them pressure.

The Moon in Virgo can be uncomfortable on a sexual level, self-critical and can have body issues and can be uneasy with their sexuality, but they are nonetheless pleasers. When a Lunar Virgo discovers their bloom, they become more open as partners with a lot to share. They are kind people who are shy lovers.

Lunar Virgos are skeptics and wonder at the blind faith others carry happily with them. They can be vocally critical of people who can't see the practical in situations and this can be maddening for those who like to dream and wish and hope for the best. Because of the practicality that drives them, they can seem hardened to the sensitive personality. They show interest in other people's problems but seem to wane in interest after, because practicality takes over. When they give advice it is blunt and straight-forward - practical. But they are sensitive to other people's criticism and surprisingly fragile when they feel that they are under the microscope.

When their lives are under control, this is when the Lunar Virgo is happiest. All they want is to live a quiet existence and live simple. So long as they are able to manage the little things in their lives, then all is well with the Moon in Virgo and they are delightful company.

THE MOON IN LIBRA

Partnership is important to the Moon in Libra; this is when they feel absolutely secure and complete. Lunar Librans are the type of people who would drag you along even if it were to the corner store to get some milk. They are happiest when they feel a warm hand engulf theirs. They are driven by sharing, peace and harmony so much so that they are usually some of your friends who decide to live together or get married early. They need to share their lives with someone and to feel wanted. They are observant and see the faults not only in their relationships, selves but also the community and environment they live in. If they can do something about it, they will.

The Moon in Libra is refined, gentle and a big flirt. People, men, women and children, gravitate toward them because they are charming beings who are not only attentive of you; they listen and are quite attractive to be around. Despite their penchant for giving in to things, Lunar Librans love a good conversation and revel in intelligent debates. A mental connection is important to them. They thrive on mental stimulation hence they are also good socializers.

The Moon in Libra is always the first one to show concern and sympathy. They are idealistic individuals who have a clear idea of how they want to live and this could distract them from living in the moment, questing for a better way. The Lunar Libran keeps their opinions to themselves around large groups and acquaintances, saving debates and discussions with their partners. Although reserved with their words, but a quick with humor and light jokes, the charming life of the party Moon in Libra, will always work their way around a conversation and win in a private debate with their partners.

You will sometimes feel like you're under inquest when the Lunar Libran sits and has a talk with you, but you will always find the Moon in Libra the first to defend you and support your point of view when you least expect it.

THE MOON IN SCORPIO

Leave it up to the Moon in Scorpio to seek out experiences to stimulate their inner selves. Uneasy with the mundane the Lunar Scorpio will not think twice about pushing their limits and setting new heights. They have a rooted need to transform and renew themselves in various ways for different individuals. Their lives are some of the most emotionally charged and intense. They seem to be magnets for inner upheaval and lead lives like the motion of a rollercoaster. The Lunar Scorpio is not one to find their security in accumulating things but they seek out emotional stimulation.

You can't get one past the Lunar Scorpio because they are able to see through and cut right into the core of a person. To some this trait of the Lunar Scorpio can become scary whilst to others, a visceral attraction. The Moon in Scorpio has a deep strong fear of being betrayed and will proactively seek the spoken and felt commitment of a partner, almost to the point of having the partner give up something for them. Never one to not go the distance and the whole nine yards, the Lunar Scorpio gives it all or nothing. Meaningless relations are not something the Moon in Scorpio will waste time on.

They unconsciously would test the people they love for their fealty and this could be tiresome and trying for those they love to go through a needle's eye to ward off suspicion but once they understand your deep commitment to them they are the most loyal, caring, loving partners. They have great intuition and can sense things more strongly than others. They spend a lot of their energy in controlling their seemingly tireless emotion driven quest for intensity. They are pillars of strength who possess great wisdom for many things. You can count on a Moon in Scorpio to feel your mood shift, your emotional turmoil and they will not be the sort to back away from anyone who approaches them for emotional honesty.

Most people will find themselves magnetically drawn to a Moon in Scorpio to confide whilst other run the other way. They are exceptional judges of character and are keen on sizing up the intentions of an individual. They are intelligent individuals who thrive on intimacy and honesty and make some of the best friends if you aren't scared off at the onset.

THE MOON IN SAGITTARIUS

You would swear that the word freedom and space were words invented for the spirit of the Lunar in Sagittarius. Keep them in a cubicle or cooped up and in a room and it won't take them very long to feel ill at ease. The easy going Lunar in Scorpio needs space and freedom to grow and thrive yet need a deep need to be in useful motion and doing activities simultaneously. Hence, it is not unlikely to see them traipse the world, meeting new people without ever having to ask for names. They love being on the road meeting all sorts and all kinds. These things are what stimulates the Lunar Scorpio and gives them a sense of well - being. They have a need to lend a hand and impart knowledge. They are lovers of wide open spaces and airy environments so it is not unusual to see a Lunar in Scorpios home environment to be sparse in furnishing yet airy bright and cheerful.

Don't forget to send them an invite with alarm when scheduling with them lest you get left standing on a street corner waiting for them to arrive. Lunar in Scorpios have a hard time remembering meet updates which can make them seem irresponsible. Forgetful as they may be with these things they are lovable and irresistible with their upbeat and cheerful nature. Their love for the outdoors is intense. Large open spaces invoke the Lunar in Sagittarius and it is perhaps why they are some of the most optimistic people you would meet.

Not one to be caught up in the mundane of everyday routine, the Lunar Sagittarius will make a quick getaway when things get too tough. As fleeting as they may seem there is something about their blind faith that makes them compellingly admirable.

Their deep seated belief that everything will work itself out is contagious, so much so that would you think they have a clear map in their heads about the things to come. Remember schedules? Well forget that with the Lunar in Sagittarius because they like spontaneity and spur of the moment forays. For those not as free spirited or those whose free spirit was stunted, the Lunar in Sagittarius is the one to hang out with. They are quick to adapt to changing it up and will not back down from a spontaneous side trip. Their innately passionate need to expand their horizons, widen their berth, spread their wings, learn of things new and strange things is palpable and needs to be feed.

THE MOON IN CAPRICORN

The Moon in Capricorn has a powerful urge to feel needed in the world. Productivity is what the Lunar Capricorn needs to be able to feel useful and of service. They are seldom seen to show their emotions. The Moon in

Capricorn comes off as practical and competent but in fact they are just good at hiding their emotions and prefer to take a hold and a good grip on the reins of their emotional lives. They aren't comfortable taking risks and setting up their surroundings in order to feel safe and secure takes up a lot of their time and effort.

The Moon in Capricorn is the sort who would start shopping for Christmas gifts in June. They are the ones who take care of the big-need fuels like securing their retirement or storing money away for later. They come off to be as cool as a cucumber except for when they have to deal with other people's breakdowns because they too themselves have a tendency to lose it when overpowered or filled to the brim with pent up feelings and emotions.

They become known as pillars of strength when in fact they too are just as susceptible to breaking down once in a while just as the other signs are. They are just not as showy nor are they comfortable in any display of unhinged emotions in public or outwardly. They are practical as they are efficient and will never let on unless they can't help it.

THE MOON IN AQUARIUS

You can't get one past the Moon in Aquarius because they are the really observant ones who check out everything in their surroundings and are people-analyzers. Not only do they love to people watch they are also keen observers of what makes people tick and human nature in general. They are typically quite onlookers and perhaps it is because they grow up feeling detached and different from the rest of society in general. They enjoy their own company and have no qualms about spending time on their own, but they are quite sociable as well given the right opportunity and environment. They develop defense mechanisms to survive the everyday drum of life and will work at making themselves the most standout person, unique and eclectic in their own way.

The Moon in Aquarius when young will give in to tantrums and will have their share of losing it one time or another, but as they grow they develop a more sanguine personality and find emotional displays to be an energy drainer. The Moon in Aquarius is quick to recognize the motivation and behavior in others. They feel as if they never quite fit in and this puts them in a position on the fringes. The Moon in Aquarius individual may seem distant, aloof or removed from a situation when in fact these are ways that help them deal when they feel engulfed by what they would consider to be petty emotions such as possessiveness, or jealousy.

The Lunar Aquarian is an independent soul and strives to find their individuality and unique qualities. These are the things they enhance in themselves in order to set themselves apart from the majority. You will notice a Lunar Aquarian to be of strong will even at a young age and they grow up developing this trait. They have deep love for family and will brag about their family being a unique class of their own - not that they make up stories, it is that they see the qualities and traits that make an individual person or family/tribe for their unique and distinct qualities. Careful you do not cross the path of a Lunar in Aquarius and anything derogatory about their character or you will a wall of ice go between you.

They are sensitive to criticism most especially when they feel that they have been character attacked. See them go about coolly still doing what it is they were called out on. They have high expectations of people around them accepting them the way they are as do they - otherwise be ready to get cut out. They are charming and often unpredictable sort who can be bullish and stubborn. The Moon in Aquarius is quite the independent one and would sometimes seem that they are detached, cold, unfeeling or distant at times but this is only because they have faith that the rest of the people around them are able rise above and be as independent as they are.

They are tolerant, open-minded beings who welcome the quirks and intricateness of the people who surround them giving those individuals the freedom to be who they are when they around the Moon in Aquarius. They may come off as people who give little care to the mundane things we deal with on a day to day basis. However, if you get the opportunity to know them well enough you will discover that they give the same freedom of space to those they love and care for as they would allow themselves. Being a fixed sign, even if they do seem flighty, they are in fact, on the whole, loyal and trustworthy.

A great advocate and an ally, they make really good friends. They are the ones who will welcome a new face into a group and go out of their way to make people feel included. They are great advocators of equality.

THE MOON IN PISCES

Amongst one of the many endearing qualities of the Moon in Pisces is that they are easy going people who are perceptive individuals and may seem a bit off and spaced out at times. The Lunar Pisces are true blue friends who don't pipe up too often but are always attentive - they're the ones who listen and laugh at the right times. They are remarkably intuitive people who have a great sense of empathy often losing themselves in other people's sorrow. This is another of their endearing traits because they show such great compassion and unmistakably, love. The dreamer in the Lunar Pisces may not be up to date with going on in and around the world as others are but what they lack in that area they make up for with great compassion for others. The Lunar Pisces needs space and time to regress and be on their own and just be oblivious to the world, they need to detach and dream away. Given the space they need the unconventional Moon in Pisces will be able to reconnect better.

They are easily swayed by human conditions and this shows in their soft hearted manner. Although they do have plenty of soft corners and they are rapt listeners of problematic stories of others, they are intuitive about people who are simply out to manipulate and they can tell when a person is sincere. Being the twelfth and last sign of the zodiac, the Lunar Pisces carries a bit of the traits of all the other signs therefore they are able to see a bit of themselves in other people they come across, people around them and random passersby in their lives.

Great compassion and an attitude of embrace is what they have for all. They are able to put themselves in other people's shoes and understand what a person goes through even without having gone through it themselves. They are open - minded human beings with great hearts to boot. A Lunar in Pisces is creative and has a need to express themselves through art in one form or another. Whether it be acting, writing, listening to, creating or writing music, poetry, drawing, painting, crafting, the Moon in Pisces individual is the happiest when given freedom to be able to express themselves this way. They need short, solitary, alone - time to regroup and recharge away from the realities of the routine in their world.

Chapter Ten: Conclusion and Points to Remember

Whether on a quest to know more about your inner workings or to quench your thirst for more knowledge on the subject, we hope that we have whet your appetite enough for you to press on and discover more. There are more ancient studies of astronomy to discover if it interests you to know. Many countries in our modern world today still use the principles of astronomy and swear by it. Medicine, Architecture, Engineering, are some of the fields of today's world which still consult the heavens for clues and responses to questions.

While an astrologer will be able to help read and interpret your chart and give connection to what is happening up yonder and how these relate here below you mustn't begin to think that they are right all the time. They too are human. You and your astrologer should be able to work together well in order to have a clear understanding and to set expectations. In the end the information they give you in order to aid you in making good decisions and coming up with the best solutions to your situation is left to you. No one can make a decision for you and you should not leave this up to anyone else but yourself.

We hope that we have been able to shed a little more light on the subject and became instrumental in learning a little more about people around you but most of all, yourself. There is no good or bad in the stars, just signs and wonders a select few will choose to follow. It is the results of our actions we should be concerned about - never not care about the outcome of your actions. You may find it hard to trust, forgive and believe in yourself if you do. The quest to find one is an innate, visceral need each one of us possesses, but only a few will act on it. Choose wisely.

Key Points to Remember

Facts about Astrology

- Astrology is a mathematical study of the placement and alignment of the planets, and how the pull of the Sun and the Moon on the Earth along with its pull of the stars and planets affects and affects one's birth date and time.

- This is a subject that deals with the stars, planets and their celestial dance of movements which co-relates to events on the earth and on affairs specific to individual humans.

- Astrology narrows down and relates to each individual even more when consideration is taken upon the 12 signs of the zodiac, each with their own combination of the 4 Element qualities unique to a sign.

- The 12 signs are subdivided into 4 groups which are earth, fire, water and air. Libra, Gemini and Aquarius fall under the sign of Air; Leo, Sagittarius, Aries fall under the Fire sign; Pisces, Cancer, Scorpio fall under the Water sign and Virgo, Taurus, Capricorn make up the Earth sign.

- There are many classifications of the discipline of astrology from business astrology, to medical astrology and these are two categories studied and practiced for reasons relating to finances and health.

- The traditional Chinese, Vietnamese, Japanese and Bon and Hindu Astrology deals with Five elements namely; Fire, Air, Water, Earth and Void whereas Western Astrology follows the four classical elements of Fire, Water, Earth, and Air.

12 Houses of Zodiac and their Moon Significance

The House of Aries

- The First House is Aries and is ruled by the planet Mars. Aries rules over the head.

- The Moon over Aries is passionate on, with the need to blaze on as it contemplates, searches, and experiments to gain results. The quicker the better! Feelings are cast aside and activity and movement masks having to deal with sentiments anew to them. The Moon over Aries is one with a temper.

The House of Taurus

- Taurus is a feminine sign. It is the first Earth sign as well as the first fixed sign. This House is ruled by Venus. Taurus resides in the throat and neck.

- Having any sort of close relationship to a Moon in Taurus gives those closest to them a comfort in their steadiness. Intimacy and familiarity is vital to the strong-willed Moon Taurean.

The House of Gemini

- Gemini lords over all kinds of communication forms. This house also is relative to siblings, schools, community affairs, local travel and neighborhoods.
- Moon in Gemini are people who are curious about almost anything and have a great ability to gain and store information. They are great talkers, thinkers and readers. The Lunar Gemini is charming as they are clever and quick with a joke or a smart remark.

The House of Cancer

- The House of Cancer deals with mothering traits of nurturing. The birthstone of Cancer is the moonstone. They are perfect for dealing with antiquities, are good archeologists, suitable in the catering or hotel business.

- The Lunar Cancer is one who shows great promise in sensing and recognizing emotional changes people go through when they themselves are often wrapped up in their own world.

The House of Leo

- Leo governs the eyes, spine, and the heart. It governs creativeness in the individual as it rules over self-expression, attention as well as play and recreational fun. It is a Masculine sign.

- The Lunar Leo likes to take control of things and take charge of their domain. They are the sort who require lots of affection and showered with tons of TLC to operate at an optimum level.

The House of Virgo

- It lords over routines, diet and exercising, healthy living the natural and simple way. They are in-service to others and are good in ruling schedules and have good organizational skills.

- Lunar Virgos for lack of wanting to put themselves out there have been called unambitious and lacking in self-confidence but in fact this is what they know to be themselves and take pride in living simply and in the background giving support.

The House of Libra

- It is the house which lords over the personally binding relationships and business partnerships which come with a contract in shared-relations involving enemies, marriage, divorce, fights, and lawsuits.

- The Moon in Libra is refined, gentle and a big flirt. People, men, women and children, gravitate toward them because they are charming beings who are not only attentive of you; they listen and are quite attractive to be around.

The House of Scorpio

- It rules over monies and possessions i.e. property, investments and inheritance. They are known for their aggressive nature which can be impulsive aiding the change of any event they are dealing with.

- Leave it up to the Moon in Scorpio to seek out experiences to stimulate their inner selves. Uneasy with the mundane the Lunar Scorpio will not think twice about pushing their limits and setting new heights.

The House of Sagittarius

- They are known for their optimism. Sagittarius individuals aim for higher learning and foreign languages.

- For those not as free spirited or those whose free spirit was stunted, the Lunar in Sagittarius is the one to hang out with. They are quick to adapt to changing it up and will not back down from a spontaneous side trip.

The House of Pisces

- Pisceans are inspirational individuals that tend to be good in higher learning. They gain increased knowledge through learning and are driven by their ethics and morality.

- The Lunar Pisces are true blue friends who don't pipe up too often but are always attentive - they're the ones who listen and laugh at the right times. They are remarkably intuitive people who have a great sense of empathy often losing themselves in other people's sorrow.

The House of Capricorn

- They seem reserved as they ponder on decisions and are careful to respond, mindful of the environment around them.

- The Moon in Capricorn has a powerful urge to feel needed in the world. Productivity is what the Lunar Capricorn needs to be able to feel useful and of service. They are seldom seen to show their emotions.

The House of Aquarius

- They are suited for projects aiming for the betterment of their communities.

  - You can't get one past the Moon in Aquarius because they are the really observant ones who check out everything in their surroundings and are people-analyzers.

Photo Credits

Page 1 Photo by user Quique via Pixabay,
https://pixabay.com/en/horoscope-sign-zodiac-96309/

Page 2 Photo by user Geralt via Pixabay,
https://pixabay.com/en/star-constellation-universe-bull-2630050/

Page 9 Photo by user Alexas Fotos via Pixabay,
https://pixabay.com/en/starry-sky-zodiac-sign-clock-2533021/

Page 17 Photo by user darkmoon1968 via Pixabay,
https://pixabay.com/en/aquarius-zodiac-sign-horoscope-2689948/

Page 24 Photo by user darkmoon1968 via Pixabay,
https://pixabay.com/en/aries-zodiac-sign-horoscope-2689949/

Page 28 Photo by user darkmoon1968 via Pixabay,
https://pixabay.com/en/cancer-zodiac-sign-horoscope-2689033/

References

The Career Astrologer – Quarterly Magazine -
Opaastrology.org
https://www.opaastrology.org/publications/career-
astrologer/94-becoming-an-astrologer

Understanding Astrology - Astrology.com
https://www.astrology.com/us/articles/understanding-
astrology.aspx

First steps in Astrology - Astro.com
An Introduction not only for kids
http://www.astro.com/astrology/in_kdfstep_e.htm

What is Vedic Hindu Astrology? - Thoughtco.com
https://www.thoughtco.com/what-is-vedic-astrology-
1770025

Ruling Planets of Zodiac Signs - Thoughtco.com
https://www.thoughtco.com/ruling-planets-of-zodiac-signs-
206734

Astrology - Wikipedia.org
https://en.wikipedia.org/wiki/Astrology

Zodiac Signs And Astrology Signs Meanings And Characteristics - Astrology-Zodiac-Signs.com
http://www.astrology-zodiac-signs.com/

How to Make Sense Of Your Birth Chart - Refinery29.com
http://www.refinery29.com/2016/11/129929/birth-chart-analysis-natal-astrology-reading

Learning to Interpret Birth Charts - Thoughtco.com
https://www.thoughtco.com/taurus-rising-rising-signs-p2-207238

Introduction to Astrology - Astro.com
http://www.astro.com/astrology/in_intro_e.htm

Houses - Astro.com
http://www.astro.com/astrology/in_house2_e.htm

First Steps in Astrology - Astro.com
http://www.astro.com/astrology/in_kdfstep_e.htm

What are Moon Signs? - AlwaysAstrology.com
http://www.alwaysastrology.com/moon-signs.html

Influence of the Moon on Your Astrological Sign - Thoughtco.com
https://www.thoughtco.com/the-moon-sign-206731

What is Astrology? - AlwaysAstrology.com

http://www.alwaysastrology.com/learn-astrology.html

Feeding Baby
Cynthia Cherry
978-1941070000

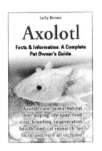

Axolotl
Lolly Brown
978-0989658430

Dysautonomia, POTS
Syndrome
Frederick Earlstein
978-0989658485

Degenerative Disc
Disease Explained
Frederick Earlstein
978-0989658485

Sinusitis, Hay Fever,
Allergic Rhinitis Explained
Frederick Earlstein
978-1941070024

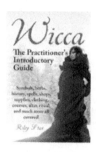

Wicca
Riley Star
978-1941070130

Zombie Apocalypse
Rex Cutty
978-1941070154

Capybara
Lolly Brown
978-1941070062

Eels As Pets
Lolly Brown
978-1941070167

Scabies and Lice Explained
Frederick Earlstein
978-1941070017

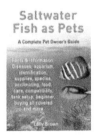

Saltwater Fish As Pets
Lolly Brown
978-0989658461

Torticollis Explained
Frederick Earlstein
978-1941070055

Kennel Cough
Lolly Brown
978-0989658409

Physiotherapist, Physical
Therapist
Christopher Wright
978-0989658492

Rats, Mice, and Dormice
As Pets
Lolly Brown
978-1941070079

Wallaby and Wallaroo Care
Lolly Brown
978-1941070031

Bodybuilding Supplements
Explained
Jon Shelton
978-1941070239

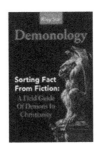

Demonology
Riley Star
978-19401070314

Pigeon Racing
Lolly Brown
978-1941070307

Dwarf Hamster
Lolly Brown
978-1941070390

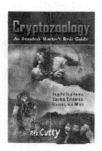

Cryptozoology
Rex Cutty
978-1941070406

Eye Strain
Frederick Earlstein
978-1941070369

Inez The Miniature Elephant
Asher Ray
978-1941070353

Vampire Apocalypse
Rex Cutty
978-1941070321

Made in the USA
Monee, IL
19 June 2023

36216899R00063